# Beyond the Shadow of the Mind: A Positive Journey through Mental Illness

# Preface

Welcome to an unprecedented journey through the intricate depths of the human mind. In this book, we will immerse ourselves in a courageous and enlightening exploration of mental illnesses, not as insurmountable barriers, but as secret doors leading to extraordinary personal growth.

Our modern society is often plagued by degenerative mental illnesses, but it is time to transform our perception of them. This is not just a manual for understanding; it is a guide to embracing mental diversity as a unique opportunity for self-discovery and growth.

From the introductory chapter, challenging the conventional view of mental illnesses, to the exploration of "depressionism" as a signal of necessary change, every page is an invitation to look beyond the apparent surface.

Through a journey that addresses Alzheimer's as an accumulation of useless memory and anxiety as an engine for personal growth, we will discover that behind every symptom lies a potential key to our development.

At the heart of the book, we will learn the art of introspection and the reverse engineering of mental illnesses, revealing how these conditions can become springboards for positive change. We will accept and embrace mental diversity, breaking the patterns of "normality" to embrace the richness of our diverse humanity.

Living in the present and cultivating resilience become imperatives to prevent self-induced suffocation from mental illnesses. As we explore bipolar disorder as a natural cycle of emotions and address eating disorders with a positive approach, we will discover that the key to vibrant mental health may lie in the active management of these experiences.

In the final section, we will approach the conclusion with a reminder of the importance of embracing mental challenges as vehicles for personal growth. We will look to the future by imagining a society that celebrates mental diversity, where mental health is as highly valued as physical health.

This book is a call to action for all those who want to break free from the chains of negative perception of mental illnesses. Through understanding, acceptance, and positive transformation, we can embark on an extraordinary journey toward a healthy mind and a meaningful life. Be ready to explore the unexplored and discover the bright potential beyond the shadow of the mind.

# Chapter 1: Introduction

The human mind, intricate and marvelous, is an unexplored universe of emotions, thoughts, and memories. However, this complex inner landscape can be the stage for significant challenges—mental illnesses. In an era where the pressures of daily life accumulate, and tensions become increasingly palpable, mental health emerges as a critical milestone for our overall well-being.

## Discovering Our Inner World

Modern times confront us with a paradigm where degenerative mental illnesses are commonplace, threatening our emotional balance. Yet, instead of approaching this topic with fear or resignation, we are about to embark on a journey of discovery and transformation. This book is an illuminating guide, a beacon in the night of mental illnesses, but above all, it is a key to open the door to deep and meaningful personal growth.

## From Suffering to Opportunity

The traditional perspective on mental illnesses often leads us to consider them as curses, but what if we view them as opportunities for growth? This book embraces the bold idea that behind every mental challenge lies an opportunity to explore, learn, and grow. The intention is to flip the paradigm, shifting our gaze from suffering to the discovery of internal resources and unexpected possibilities.

## An Enlightening Approach

Understanding mental illnesses requires more than a simple analysis of symptoms. We must adopt an open and positive approach, shedding light on the often overlooked aspects of our psyche. This book serves as a guide, taking us through uncharted territory of introspection and retrospective analysis. We will explore how the mind tackles challenges, discovering how we can transform these challenges into vehicles for personal growth.

## A Commitment to Universal Mental Well-being

Our commitment is universal. We address not only those actively facing mental illnesses but all those who wish to understand, support, and promote vibrant mental health. Through this journey, we not only cast a new light on mental illnesses but also cultivate fertile ground for awareness, understanding, and acceptance of mental diversity.

**Next Stop: Exploring the Roots of Alzheimer's**

Our first step will lead us to examine Alzheimer's, not as an isolated illness but as a symptom of a deeper issue. We will explore the excessive storage of useless memory as a key to understanding how our minds process and retain information. Prepare for a dive into the complexity of our memory and the opportunity to shape our perception of the past to create a brighter future.

Our journey has just begun, an invitation to embrace knowledge and transform our relationship with mental illnesses into an experience of growth and awareness. Welcome aboard.

# Chapter 2: Alzheimer as Excessive Accumulation of Unnecessary Memory

**Unveiling the Secrets of the Mind: A Journey into Alzheimer's**

Alzheimer's, often considered a dark enigma, becomes our guide through the mysterious territory of the human mind. In this chapter, we don't view Alzheimer's as an isolated illness but as an intricate labyrinth of memory and perception. The key to unlocking its mystery? Exploring the excessive accumulation of unnecessary memory.

**Memory: A Double-Edged Sword**

Memory, the jewel of our mind, can reveal itself as a double-edged sword. While it allows us to preserve the treasures of our most precious memories, it can also become a trap where seemingly useless information accumulates. In this context, Alzheimer's emerges as a distorted response to an excess of mnemonic "baggage."

## The Invisible Weight of Superfluous Memories

Imagine our memory as an archive, a personal library of experiences and knowledge. However, as we navigate through life, not everything we store is of equal value. Some information, insignificant or even harmful, accumulates like dust on neglected shelves. Alzheimer's could be seen as our brain's response to this overload, a distorted attempt to "clean up" the excessive chaos.

## The Vicious Cycle of Mental Overcrowding

What makes Alzheimer's so fascinating is its relationship with our daily memory management. How we handle information every day can have profound implications for our long-term mental health. The accumulation of irrelevant details, the weight of insignificant events, the constant overload of our memory contribute to creating a fertile ground for conditions like Alzheimer's.

## Filtering for Mental Clarity

The goal, therefore, becomes clear: learning to filter, to discern what is truly meaningful. This is not just a mental exercise but an act of preserving our mental health. An active selection process that promotes mental clarity, leaving space only for memories that enrich our lives and contribute to our well-being.

## Freeing the Mind from Unnecessary Weight

Trapped in a whirlwind of superfluous memories, we risk suffocating our minds. However, by recognizing Alzheimer's as a response to this suffocation, we gain transformative power. We can learn to free our minds from unnecessary weight, adopting daily practices that promote a focus on what truly matters.

## Beyond Alzheimer's: A New Approach to Memory

Exploring Alzheimer's in this way opens doors to a new approach to memory. Not as a passive repository but as a garden that requires care and attention. Learning to cultivate our memory consciously becomes crucial to prevent unnecessary overload and promote a free, agile, and healthy mind.

**An Invitation to Reflect**

In conclusion, this chapter is an invitation to reflect on the nature of our memory and its connection to mental well-being. As we explore Alzheimer's as a response to information overload, we are called to become active custodians of our minds. The next step? Deepening our understanding of mnemonic dynamics and adopting daily practices to free our minds from unnecessary weight, thus promoting vibrant and enduring mental health.

# Chapter 3: Memory as a Source of Personal Growth

## Illuminating Memory: An Unexplored Resource

Memory, often considered a treasure trove of recollections, lies at the heart of our journey toward personal growth. In this chapter, we will delve into the concept of memory not as a burden to bear but as an unexplored source, a potential catalyst for our individual evolution.

### Memory: Burden or Catalyst?

The notion of memory as a burden may stem from the passive accumulation of experiences. However, what we propose is a revolutionary perspective: to see memory as an active tool that can be cultivated and used to fuel our personal growth. Not a weight to drag along, but a dynamic resource that accompanies us on our path of self-discovery.

## Advanced Memory Management Techniques

We explore advanced memory management techniques, not just to recall past events but to use memory as a tool for learning, adapting, and growing. Through practical exercises, readers will be guided in creating an intentional approach to memory, learning to select and nurture memories that contribute to their personal development.

## Present-Focused: A Bridge Between Memory and Growth

The key to transforming the perception of memory lies in present-focused attention. As we look back, we do so with a clear purpose: to learn and grow in the present. Memory thus becomes a bridge between our past and our future, a place to draw wisdom and knowledge to shape our present meaningfully.

## Memory as a Life Teacher

Memory becomes a life teacher, guiding us through the lessons learned from the highs and lows of our journey. We acknowledge challenging moments as learning opportunities, depositing in our memory not only successes but also difficulties as essential pieces for our growth.

## The Unexplored Potential of Emotional Memory

We also explore the unexplored potential of emotional memory. Emotions tied to our memories can serve as powerful catalysts for personal growth. Through a profound understanding of our emotional responses to memories, we can consciously shape our present and future experiences.

## Creativity in the Architecture of Memory

Creativity plays a fundamental role in the architecture of memory. We examine how we can use creativity to shape our memories positively, transforming them into works of art that enrich our understanding of ourselves and the world around us.

## A New Paradigm: Memory and Synergistic Growth

In conclusion, we present a new paradigm: the synergy between memory and personal growth. Memory is no longer just a treasure chest but becomes the fertile ground where we plant the seeds of our continuous evolution. Readers are invited to explore this synergistic connection, recognizing in memory not only a custodian of

the past but also a valuable guide
on our constant journey toward
an enhanced version of ourselves.

**Next Stop: Anxiety as a Engine
for Personal Growth**

We conclude this chapter by
opening the door to an exciting
next stop: anxiety as an engine
for personal growth. Through a
profound understanding of the
nuances of this emotion, readers
will be guided toward new
horizons of self-discovery and
personal development.

# Chapter 4: The Art of Introspection and Reverse Engineering of Mental Illnesses

## The Mirror of the Soul: Introspection as the Key

The art of introspection is like a magical mirror that allows us to peer into the soul, revealing the profound intricacies of our minds. In this chapter, we not only explore introspection as a skill to cultivate but also as a beacon that illuminates the roots of mental illnesses.

## The Practice of Introspection: A Powerful Tool

Introspection, often overlooked in the hustle of daily life, becomes our ally. We introduce practical tools to cultivate this skill, inviting readers to dedicate moments of mindful reflection to explore the recesses of their psyche. The goal is not only to understand but also to transform.

## Reverse Engineering: Unveiling Hidden Mechanisms

Let's go further, embracing reverse engineering as an illuminating methodology. We tackle mental illnesses as engineers of the mind, dismantling the complex mechanisms that fuel them. Understanding the roots becomes essential for undertaking lasting transformation.

## From Symptoms to Cause: A New Paradigm

We often focus on the symptoms of mental illnesses without exploring their profound causes. Reverse engineering offers a deeper insight, transforming how we perceive and treat mental conditions. It's not just about managing symptoms but tracing back to the very root.

## Tailored Preventive and Therapeutic Strategies

With reverse engineering as our compass, we develop tailored strategies. We observe how certain thought patterns, past experiences, or specific situations intertwine with mental illnesses. This not only paves the way for preventive strategies but also for personalized therapies, respecting the uniqueness of each individual.

## Authenticity as an Antidote

Introspection and reverse engineering lead us to authenticity. As we explore the roots of mental illnesses, we also venture into the terrain of our authenticity. Embracing who we truly are becomes a fundamental part of the transformation process, an antidote to the forces that fuel mental illnesses.

## Transforming Obsessions into Opportunities

Obsessions, often associated with conditions like obsessive-compulsive disorder, can become vehicles of transformation. In this chapter, we learn to reverse engineer obsessions, turning them into opportunities for growth and self-discovery.

## A Map for Self-Discovery

The chapter also serves as a map for self-discovery. We encourage readers to explore the recesses of their minds, to chart a course through their experiences, emotions, and thoughts. Reverse engineering becomes the compass guiding them on this inner journey.

**Next Stop: Embracing Mental Diversity**

We conclude the chapter by opening the doors to the next stop on our journey: accepting and embracing mental diversity. We are ready to explore how reverse engineering can illuminate the path to acceptance, promoting an inclusive and compassionate view of the human mind.

# Chapter 5: Embracing and Celebrating Mental Diversity

## The Harmony of the Mind: Celebrating Diversity as the Norm

In this chapter, we delve into the essence of the human experience, revealing the intrinsic truth that mental diversity is the norm, not the exception. We abandon the outdated notion of "normality" to embrace the harmony that arises from the vastness of the human mind.

## Breaking the Chains of Judgment

We cease to perceive mental illnesses as "anomalies." This limiting attitude is a barrier to understanding and connection. Instead, we open the door to awareness, embracing the diverse nuances of the human mind without preconceptions or judgments. Diversity becomes a richness to explore, not a reason for alienation.

**The Unexplored Power of Unique Perspectives**

Each mind is an unexplored universe. We explore how the unique perspectives brought by mental illnesses enrich our understanding of the world. From depression to bipolarity, each condition brings with it a lens through which we can rediscover the beauty and complexity of life.

**From "Normality" to Inclusivity**

We embrace inclusivity as the new standard. We dismantle the illusion of a monolithic "normality," embracing mental diversity as a fundamental part of the human experience. In an inclusive world, everyone contributes to the mosaic of society, bringing a unique value that transcends the limitations of labels.

## Mental Diversity as a Driving Force

We reflect on mental diversity not only as an individual characteristic but also as a driving force for innovation and creativity. We explore stories of individuals who have transformed mental challenges into sources of inspiration, demonstrating that mental diversity can be the fertile ground for genius and resilience.

## Overcoming Stereotypes and Stigma

We confront the stereotypes and stigma associated with mental illnesses. Understanding and accepting mental diversity require breaking conceptual barriers. We encourage society to overcome the fear of the unknown, educate itself on the complexity of the mind, and challenge limiting labels.

## The Power of Empathy

Empathy becomes the key to open hearts and minds. We invite readers to walk in the shoes of others, to understand the challenges that mental illnesses can bring. Through empathy, we build bridges of understanding, demonstrating that mental diversity is a precious resource, not a burden.

## Celebrating Differences as a Revolutionary Act

We conclude the chapter by celebrating differences as a revolutionary act. We are ready to redefine the concept of normality, to embrace diversity as a source of strength and wisdom. We look to the future with the awareness that accepting and embracing mental diversity is the foundation for a more compassionate and inclusive society. Diversity becomes the melody that unites the unique voices of each individual in a harmonious choir, celebrating the beauty of the human mind in all its nuances.

# Chapter 6: Living in the Present and Cultivating Resilience

## The Power of the "Here and Now"

In the whirlwind of modern life, we often forget the power of the present. In this chapter, we will unveil the profound meaning of living in the "here and now." Learning to connect with the present moment becomes a crucial antidote to the self-imposed suffocation of mental illnesses.

## Mindfulness: The Path to Awareness

We introduce mindfulness as a key practice. Through exercises and techniques, readers will be guided to develop acute awareness of their mental state and daily experiences.

Mindfulness becomes the beacon that illuminates the path through the chaos of the mind, offering refuge in the present.

## Breaking the Chains of the Past and Future

We explore how the mind, often imprisoned by past regrets and future fears, can find freedom in the present. We invite readers to recognize the weight of worries that keep them tethered to the past or future, encouraging them to break these mental chains and immerse themselves in the beauty of the present.

## Resilience as an Essential Skill

We address resilience as a fundamental key to navigating life's challenges. Not a quality reserved for a chosen few, but a skill that can be cultivated by everyone. We will illustrate how to transform difficulties into opportunities for personal growth through a resilient mindset.

## The Art of Accepting the Inevitable

A crucial element of resilience is accepting the inevitable. We explore how welcoming events, even painful or unexpected ones, can unleash a reserve of inner strength. Acceptance does not mean surrender; it means embracing reality with courage and wisdom.

## Transforming Challenges into Opportunities

Every challenge carries a disguised opportunity. We will illustrate stories of resilience, where individuals have turned adversity into catalysts for growth. From loss to failure, we will explore how every difficulty can become fertile ground for the sprout of resilience.

## Resilience as a Process, Not a Outcome

Contrary to common perception, resilience is not a destination but a continuous process. We invite readers to understand that resilience develops in the journey, not at the end. This perspective opens the way to constant growth and evolving strength.

## The Importance of Social Support

We explore the fundamental role of social support in cultivating resilience. Supportive relationships become anchors that sustain during life's storms. We encourage the building of support networks, revealing how connecting with others can be a source of inspiration and strength.

## Living Each Day as a New Opportunity

We conclude the chapter by emphasizing the importance of approaching each day as a new opportunity for growth and change. The art of living in the present, coupled with resilience, becomes a powerful elixir for a healthy and robust mind. We look to the future with the awareness that cultivating resilience and living in the present are the keys to a fulfilling and meaningful life.

# Chapter 7: Depressionism: A Positive View of Depression

## Rewriting the Narrative of Depression

Depression, often seen only as a dark tunnel, becomes, in our approach, a signal to decipher. In this chapter, we delve into "depressionism," a new way of perceiving depression as a catalyst for positive change.

## Depression as a Symptom of Emotional Imbalances

We address depression as a symptom speaking to our emotional being. We explore the roots of emotional imbalances, recognizing that depression is a powerful signal from our body inviting us to delve deeper into our emotional life.

## Retrospective Analysis as the Key to Understanding

Conduct an illuminating retrospective on depression. We examine how past experiences, interpersonal relationships, and personal expectations can influence our current emotional state. Depression becomes a reflection, an opportunity to look within ourselves to identify areas for necessary change.

## The Call to Change

Depression, rather than a condemnation, becomes a messenger inviting us to reconsider our lifestyle. We analyze how aspects like daily routines, interpersonal relationships, and recreational activities can be reformulated to promote emotional well-being. Depression becomes a call to change and a guide to building a healthier balance.

**Rethinking Interpersonal Relationships**

We explore the link between depression and interpersonal relationships. How can relational dynamics be transformed to become sources of support and emotional nourishment? We see depression as an opportunity to improve the quality of connections with others.

**Depression as a Push for Personal Growth**

We reconsider depression as an invitation to personal growth. Through a positive lens, we explore how emotional challenges can become fertile ground for increased self-awareness and self-understanding. Depression becomes the starting point for a journey of inner transformation.

Practical Strategies for Positive Change

We provide the reader with practical strategies to initiate the process of positive change. From adopting healthy daily habits to seeking professional support, we guide the reader through a path that transforms depression from an adversary into an ally in the pursuit of lasting well-being.

**Breaking Stereotypes about Depression**

We address cultural stereotypes related to depression. As a society, we often mislabel those who experience depression. We encourage breaking these stereotypes, promoting a deeper and more compassionate understanding of depression as an individual path toward positive change.

## Depression as a Guide to Balance

We conclude the chapter by emphasizing the importance of embracing depression as a guide to a healthier balance. A positive view of depression becomes a key to opening doors toward personal transformation. We look to the future with optimism, aware that depressionism can be a path to embracing life with a renewed and positive perspective.

# Chapter 8: Anxiety as an Engine for Personal Growth

## Rewriting the Narrative of Anxiety

Anxiety, often demonized as an adversary to our mental health, becomes, in our approach, a powerful ally for personal growth. In this chapter, we explore the role of anxiety as an engine that can guide us toward deeper awareness and the development of a resilient mindset.

## Anxiety as a Symptom of Opportunities

We begin by disarming anxiety from its role as an enemy. We see it as a signal from the body, an alarm bell indicating the need to explore hidden aspects of ourselves. Anxiety becomes a symptom not only of present worries but of opportunities for personal growth.

## Deep Analysis of Fears and Concerns

We confront the roots of anxiety, digging deeper into the fears and concerns it carries. Through profound analysis, we learn to recognize the growth potential in every anxiety we experience. We view the anxious process as a vehicle for better understanding our hidden needs and desires.

## Building a Resilient Mindset

We examine how anxiety can become fertile ground for building a resilient mindset. Through grappling with challenges, we learn to develop emotional resilience. Anxiety becomes our personal coach to face adversity with courage and determination.

## Self-Acceptance and Self-Awareness

We promote self-acceptance during the anxious process. We teach to recognize and embrace emotions without judgment, creating space for a deeper self-awareness. Anxiety becomes fertile ground for inner growth, leading to the discovery of hidden resources and inner strength.

## Anxiety as a Guide to Opportunities

We explore how anxiety can serve as a guide to opportunities. Instead of paralyzing us, it urges us to confront challenges with a fresh perspective. We see its role in our lives as a tool that invites us to expand our limits, embrace the unknown, and learn from every experience.

## Practical Tools for Anxiety Management

We provide the reader with practical tools to manage anxiety constructively. From breathing techniques to mindfulness, we guide the reader through practices that transform anxiety from an obstacle into a resource. The goal is to learn to dance with anxiety rather than resist it.

## Anxiety as a Traveling Companion

We conclude the chapter by emphasizing how anxiety can become a valuable traveling companion in our quest for personal growth. We look to the future with the awareness that anxiety, when approached with mindfulness and resilience, can become a key element for a richer and more meaningful life.

# Chapter 9: Schizophrenia as an Expression of Creativity

## The Hidden Creativity in Mental Complexity

Schizophrenia, long labeled merely as mental instability, becomes the subject of a revolutionary analysis in this chapter. We will delve into the mental complexity of those living with this condition, exploring how it can be fertile ground for creativity rather than an obstacle.

## A Fresh Perspective on Schizophrenia

We challenge common perceptions of schizophrenia, stripping it of stigmatizing labels and opening a dialogue about its connection to creativity. Schizophrenia is not just a set of symptoms but a unique way of processing the world, a lens through which new perspectives and creative possibilities emerge.

## The Unique Processing of the World

We will explore how those living with schizophrenia process the world in unique ways. A mind that dances between the realms of reality and fantasy can generate new ideas, unexpected connections, and creative solutions. We will view schizophrenia as a gift, a way of perceiving reality that translates into an authentic expression of creativity.

## Cultivating Creativity in the Schizophrenic Experience

We will teach readers to recognize and cultivate creativity in people with schizophrenia. Through stories and case studies, we will demonstrate how the unique experiences of those living with this condition can inspire artistic works, innovations, and significant contributions to society. Creativity becomes a guiding light in the darkness of stigmatization.

## Overcoming the Taboo of Mental Illness

We will confront the taboo associated with schizophrenia, challenging the conception of mental illness as mere disability. Creativity becomes a transformative tool, allowing people with schizophrenia to overcome stereotypes and be appreciated for their valuable contributions.

## Creativity as Therapy

We will explore the therapeutic potential of creativity in the context of schizophrenia. We will see how artistic expression, writing, and other creative forms can become vehicles for self-understanding and communication with others. Creativity becomes a bridge between complex inner worlds and the external world.

**Promoting Creative Inclusivity**

We promote the idea of an inclusive environment that values and celebrates the creativity of people with schizophrenia. Art and creativity become tools for breaking down barriers, building bridges of understanding and connection. Mental diversity becomes a valuable resource for the community.

**Invitation to Rewrite the Narrative**

We conclude the chapter by inviting the reader to rewrite the narrative of schizophrenia, embracing the complexity of this condition as a unique form of creativity. We look to the future

with optimism, envisioning a
society that recognizes and
celebrates mental diversity as an
endless source of inspiration and
innovation. Schizophrenia thus
becomes a fascinating chapter in
the story of the human mind.

# Chapter 10: Eating Disorders: A Positive Approach

## Navigating the Maze of Eating Disorders

Eating disorders, often shrouded in a veil of stigmatization, become the subject of an analysis aiming to radically change the perspective. In this chapter, we shed light on the deep roots of these conditions, but with the goal of transforming the narrative from a tale of suffering to an opportunity for growth and awareness.

## Illuminating Deep Roots

We explore the deep roots of eating disorders, examining the cultural, social, and personal influences that fuel them. We confront the complexity of these conditions, recognizing that they often develop as responses to deep tensions and personal challenges.

## The Art of Retrospective Understanding

We invite readers on a journey of retrospective understanding, an exploration of the origins of eating disorders in their own experiences and the surrounding society. This deep analysis becomes the foundation for transforming the relationship with food from a a a source of anxiety to a vehicle for self-empowerment.

## Opportunities for Personal Development

We emphasize how the challenges of eating disorders can be approached as opportunities for personal development. Each step toward a healthier relationship with food becomes a step toward self-awareness, body acceptance, and understanding one's emotional needs.

## Building a Healthy Relationship with Food

We provide practices and strategies to help readers build a healthy relationship with food. Through mindful attention to body signals, understanding emotions related to eating, and promoting sustainable eating habits, we demonstrate that food can become an ally, not an enemy.

## The Beauty of Body Diversity

We challenge standardized aesthetic norms, promoting the acceptance and celebration of body diversity. Each body has its uniqueness, and the goal is to cultivate a culture that appreciates the variety of physical forms without judgment.

## Transforming Guilt into Awareness

We address the guilt often associated with eating, replacing it with awareness. We see the act of nourishment not only as a physiological need but as a form of self-love and care. Awareness becomes a guiding light on the path to a balanced relationship with food.

## Community as Support

We promote the formation of support communities, places where people can share their experiences, challenges, and successes in the journey toward a positive relationship with food. Sharing becomes a catalyst for collective strength, breaking the isolation often associated with eating disorders.

## Looking to the Future with Hope

We conclude the chapter by looking to the future with hope, envisioning a society that embraces food and body diversity. Each step toward a healthier relationship with food becomes a fundamental piece in building a world where every individual feels free to nourish themselves without fears and judgments. The table thus becomes a place of celebration, appreciation, and awareness.

# Chapter 11: Bipolarity as a Natural Cycle of Emotions

**Beyond the Surface: The Emotional Mosaic of Bipolar Disorder**

Bipolar disorder, often engulfed in prejudice and misunderstandings, takes center stage in a new narrative. In this chapter, we delve into the intricacies of its emotional world, illuminating nuances beyond the surface to reveal a mosaic rich in colors and facets.

**Reconsidering the Label**

We begin by dismantling the label of a "defect" associated with bipolar disorder. Instead, we view it as a natural variation of human emotions, a cycle that can lead to greater self-understanding and understanding of others. The goal is to free this condition from stigmatization, opening the door to a more inclusive and compassionate view.

## Navigating Extremes

We examine how navigating the extremes of bipolar disorder can teach us to manage our energies more consciously. While the world often celebrates only the moments of "high energy," we emphasize that periods of calm can be equally valuable. The natural cycle becomes a teacher of balance and emotional awareness.

## The Richness of the Human Emotional Spectrum

We explore the richness of the human emotional spectrum through the prism of bipolar disorder. We see how traversing the phases of the cycle can enrich our understanding of emotions, allowing us to develop greater empathy for others and ourselves.

# Strategies for Effective Management

We provide practical strategies for the effective management of bipolar disorder. From recognizing early signs to building a strong support network, we help readers transform this natural cycle into an opportunity for growth, learning, and maintaining lasting emotional health.

## Creativity in the Emotional Swing

We explore the connection between bipolar disorder and creativity. Many individuals with this condition manifest extraordinary artistic talents. We see how channeling creative energy during high phases and finding inspiration during calm moments can be a valuable resource.

## Beyond the Individual: The Role of Society

We conclude by examining the role of society in understanding and accepting bipolar disorder. We encourage an approach that recognizes emotional diversity as an asset rather than a threat. We challenge society to cultivate an environment where every individual, regardless of their emotional range, can thrive.

## A Fresh Start: Acceptance and Growth

We close the chapter by opening the door to a fresh start. Accepting the natural cycle of bipolar disorder becomes the key to profound personal growth. Instead of seeing it as a chain, we consider it an opportunity for continuous transformation, a dance with the richness of human emotions.

# Chapter 12: Introspection and Personal Growth

## A Deep Dive Within: The Art of Exploring One's Mind

At the core of every mental challenge lies an invitation to self-discovery. In this chapter, we immerse ourselves in the art of introspection, opening the door to a profound journey within our minds. We provide practical tools that transform mental challenges into springboards for personal growth and self-empowerment.

## The Importance of Non-Judgment

We begin by breaking down the wall of judgment. Introspection requires observation without preconceptions or criticisms. We encourage readers to explore their minds with kindness,

embracing even the darkest
aspects without fear. It is in
unconditional acceptance that the
true process of transformation
begins.

## Self-Reflection Exercises

We offer a series of practical self-
reflection exercises. These are not
just tools but gateways to a deep
understanding of oneself.
Through thoughtful questions,
guided meditations, and creative
explorations, readers will be
guided to dig beneath the surface
of their minds, revealing treasures
of awareness and emotional
mindfulness.

## Turning Challenges into Opportunities

Every dark thought, every anxiety,
and every fear become vehicles
for growth. We explain how
introspection can transform
mental challenges from
insurmountable obstacles into

precious allies. Each challenge becomes a learning opportunity, a step closer to a deeper connection with oneself.

## Self-Empowerment through Understanding

Introspection is not just an act of observation; it is an act of empowerment. We illustrate how a profound understanding of oneself is the foundation of inner strength. Through this awareness, readers will be better able to navigate through daily challenges and develop a confidence that goes beyond appearances.

## The Beauty of the Continuous Process

We conclude by emphasizing that introspection is a continuous process. Personal growth has no defined end; it is an endless journey toward self-understanding and understanding others. We encourage readers to see the beauty in continuous discovery, celebrating every step along the way.

## The Art of Living Intentionally

We close the chapter with an invitation to live intentionally. Introspection is not just a mental practice but a way of life. It becomes the art of being mindful in every moment, embracing the complexity of the human mind and transforming it into an endless source of growth and personal fulfillment.

# Chapter 13: Acceptance of Mental Diversity and Inclusivity

## Embracing the Richness of the Human Mind

In this chapter, we delve into the depth of mental diversity, recognizing its importance in the fabric of society. Our goal is to prompt reflection on the beauty and richness that arises from the diversity of mental experiences, fostering an atmosphere of universal understanding and acceptance.

## Breaking Stereotypes

We begin by challenging deeply rooted stereotypes associated with mental illnesses. We illustrate how these preconceptions can fuel social bias and limit inclusivity. We encourage readers to look beyond labels, to see each individual as a unique story, rich in nuances and potentials.

## Inclusivity in Language and Action

We explore how true inclusivity goes beyond merely acknowledging mental differences. We advocate for the adoption of respectful and mindful language capable of embracing the variety of human experiences. We emphasize the importance of concrete actions in creating an environment that celebrates mental diversity, allowing each individual to feel valued and understood.

## Empathy as a Bridge for Connection

Empathy plays a crucial role in breaking down barriers of misunderstanding. We illustrate how cultivating empathy for those experiencing diverse mental journeys can create bridges of connection. Empathetic understanding becomes a vehicle for tearing down the wall of isolation that often surrounds those struggling with mental illnesses.

**Mental Diversity as a Social Asset**

We promote the view of mental diversity as a precious asset for society. We explore how diverse mental perspectives can contribute to innovation, creativity, and social resilience. We demonstrate that a society that embraces mental diversity enjoys a wealth of unique skills and perspectives.

**Educating to Combat Stigma**

We address the persistent stigma associated with mental illnesses. We illustrate how education plays a fundamental role in overcoming prejudice. We propose mental health-focused educational programs in schools and workplaces to foster deeper understanding and a more inclusive society.

## Promoting Awareness

We conclude by encouraging the adoption of initiatives to promote awareness of mental diversity. We suggest campaigns that challenge distorted perceptions of mental illnesses and support open dialogue. Only through collective awareness can we hope to create an environment where mental diversity is accepted and celebrated.

## Vision of an Inclusive Society

We look to the future, imagining a society where mental inclusivity is the norm. We dream of a world where mental differences are welcomed as a treasure rather than a burden. We close the chapter with the hope that acceptance of mental diversity becomes a guiding light for a more compassionate and prosperous society.

# Conclusions and Future Perspectives

## Embracing the Future with Optimism

In this concluding chapter, we reflect on the journey through the intricate nuances of mental illnesses, transforming them from stigmas into opportunities for growth and understanding. The importance of approaching this path with optimism and awareness is the guiding thread that shapes our considerations.

## Personal Growth through Challenges

We emphasize how each chapter has offered a unique perspective, urging readers to reconsider mental illnesses not only as conditions but as catalysts for personal growth. Every challenge, when faced with awareness, can become a springboard for a

deeper understanding of oneself
and others.

## Turning Suffering into Strength

We revisit stories of resilience
presented, demonstrating how
adversity can be transformed into
a motivating force. Where there is
suffering, there is also the
possibility to build a stronger
foundation for mental well-being.

## The Importance of Introspection

We reaffirm the importance of
introspection as a fundamental
tool. Through exploring one's
mental experiences without
judgment, readers are guided
toward a deeper understanding of
themselves and their reactions to
life's challenges.

## Acceptance and Inclusivity

We recall the chapter dedicated
to accepting mental diversity and
promoting inclusivity. The vision
of a society that embraces and
celebrates mental differences is at
the core of our hopes for the
future.

## Education as the Key to Change

We encourage education as the
key to change. Only through
knowledge and collective
understanding can we break
down stereotypes and combat
the persistent stigma associated
with mental illnesses.

## Looking to the Future

We conclude by looking to the
future with optimism and
determination. We envision a
society where mental health is
valued as much as physical
health, where open dialogue and
empathy are commonplace.

## Call to Action

We issue a call to action, encouraging readers to be agents of change in their communities. We believe that every small step toward a more positive view of mental illnesses can have a significant impact on society as a whole.

## Thank You for Accompanying Us

We conclude by expressing our deep gratitude for accompanying us on this journey. We are confident that the shared ideas have sown seeds of understanding and hope.

## The Future of Mental Health is in Our Hands

We look to the future knowing that the fate of mental health is in the hands of each of us. With a positive vision and concrete actions, we can contribute to shaping a world where every individual can live a meaningful and fulfilling life, regardless of the mental challenges they may face. Our commitment to a more compassionate and aware society is the seed we hope to see sprout in every reader. Thank you for being part of this positive transformation.

www.ingramcontent.com/pod-product-compliance
Lightning Source LLC
Chambersburg PA
CBHW031327250726
48656CB00005B/2006